amazing baby

amazing baby

the amazing story of the
first two years of life

desmond morris

FIREFLY BOOKS

A Firefly Book

Published by Firefly Books Ltd. 2008

First printing

Publisher Cataloging-in-Publication Data (U.S.)

Morris, Desmond.
    Amazing baby : the amazing story of the first two years of life / Desmond Morris.
[192] p. : col. photos. ;   cm.
Includes index.
Summary: A discovery tour through a baby's first two years of life; from conception, to development in the womb, to birth and to early development.
ISBN-13: 978-1-55407-419-8
ISBN-10: 1-55407-419-3
1. Infants. 2. Infants — Development. I. Title.
305.232 dc22   HQ774.M665Am 2008

Library and Archives Canada Cataloguing in Publication

Morris, Desmond
    Amazing baby : the amazing story of the first two years of life / Desmond Morris.
Includes index.
ISBN-13: 978-1-55407-419-8
ISBN-10: 1-55407-419-3
    1. Infants — Development. 2. Fetus — Development. I. Title.
HQ774.M664 2008   305.232   C2008-902823-6

Published in the United States by
Firefly Books (U.S.) Inc.
P.O. Box 1338, Ellicott Station
Buffalo, New York 14205

Published in Canada by
Firefly Books Ltd.
66 Leek Crescent
Richmond Hill, Ontario L4B 1H1

Developed by Hamlyn, a division of Octopus Publishing Group Ltd
2–4 Heron Quays, London E14 4JP
Executive editor: Jane McIntosh
Senior editor: Fiona Robertson
Deputy creative director: Karen Sawyer
Designer: Janis Utton
Illustrator: Kevin Jones Associates
Picture research manager: Giulia Hetherington
Picture researcher: Sally Claxton
Production manager: Ian Paton

Printed in China

contents

foreword

The human baby is truly amazing and this book is a celebration of that fact. Many baby books have been written from the point of view of the parent, offering advice on how to look after an infant, but this one is different. Instead of giving advice, it sets out to paint an accurate portrait of the first two years of human life, as seen from the child's point of view. Armed with this information it is then up to the parent to decide how best to care for a little one – from the day of his birth, when he arrives small, vulnerable and wordless, to the day he celebrates his second birthday, already walking, talking and challenging the world.

Perhaps the most astonishing fact about a baby is that, during the nine months between conception and birth, his weight increases by a staggering 3,000 million times. As soon as he is born, this meteoric growth rate slows down dramatically, so that between birth and the end of his second year an infant will have only quadrupled in size. This may seem like an impressive growth to parents, but it is nothing compared to the astonishing development that takes place inside the womb.

an evolutionary journey

The unfolding of a baby's qualities and abilities is a complex story. His tiny body has the backing of a million years of human evolution, helping different features to develop in a special sequence. All the new baby needs now is a friendly environment in which this can happen.

Evolution has armed the infant with an irresistible appeal that ensures his parents care for him, tend him, feed him and keep him clean and warm. Even the most sophisticated adults are transformed into doting protectors when faced with the helpless bundle in their arms, staring up at them with big, questioning eyes. Bearing in mind the amount of time and effort that goes into looking after a newborn, this is just as well.

a parent's role

For human beings the parental burden is huge, lasting nearly two decades for each child, but it can also be a source of intense joy. And babies are more than just babies. They also happen to be our only certain form of immortality, in the sense that they carry on our genetic line, ensuring that our genes do not die out when we ourselves come to the end of our own lives.

The importance of a baby's first two years of life cannot be overestimated. Many of the qualities he acquires during this sensitive period mark him for life. A toddler who is provided with a rich, varied, exciting environment in which he is encouraged to start exploring, and who is treated lovingly by dependable parents, stands the very best chance of acquiring a sense of confident curiosity, creative wonder and active intelligence in later life. Nestling inside his fragile head, a newborn baby has the genetically inherited equipment that is needed for this development. All his parents have to do is to offer him the setting in which this equipment can whirr into action, allowing him to fulfill his human potential. The secret is simply to let natural loving feelings express themselves – a child needs a lot of love and complete trust in the reliability of his protectors if he is to flourish.

every child is unique

Although this book looks at the common features possessed by all babies during the first two years of their lives, it must never be forgotten that every baby is unique. Each child has a DNA that is shared by no one else on the planet – even identical twins are born with different sets of fingerprints. It is the combination of a baby's genetic makeup with her specific upbringing and environment that shapes the adult individual into which she grows.

physical variations

Parents should always bear in mind that for every child who grows and acquires skills at a particular speed, there will be another who is much slower and another who is much faster. For every child of a particular weight, there will be another who is heavier and another who is lighter. Sometimes the variations between the extremes are enormous: the heaviest birth weight ever recorded for a human baby is over 35 times as much as the lightest weight recorded. The timings for developmental milestones given in this book can therefore only be approximate.

emergence of personality

Babies also show considerable variations in personality – variations that are inborn and that are not dependent on environmental differences. Almost all parents who have had several children will tell you that, to their surprise, their little ones have turned out to have strikingly different personalities. One will be quiet and placid, another lively and sociable, another careful and industrious. One will be the helpful one, another the difficult one and yet another the clever one. And even if the children have all been brought up in much the same way and in a similar domestic environment, they will still exhibit these clear differences.

the role of DNA

Variations in appearance and personality are reminders of the fact that each of us has a unique DNA and is genetically different from every other one of the 6 billion human beings who walk the earth today. It is these variations that make us so different from the production-line humanoid robots of science-fiction nightmare. Our differences are what make life on this small planet of ours so enjoyable. But although there are thousands of tiny details in which we differ from one another, there are thousands more that make us very similar. And it is these similarities, rather than the differences, that this book is presenting.

the role of the environment

In addition to the inborn characteristics of each new baby, additional influences come from the baby's environment, especially the home in which she starts to grow up. All babies are genetically programmed to develop at more or less the same rate, but a happy home life may speed up some of these processes, while a hostile or unchallenging one may slow them down. The mental capacities of a baby who grows up in a highly stimulating world may end up being much greater than if she had been born into a harsh or boring environment.

a new baby

birth

The moment of birth comes as a great shock to a baby. Life inside the womb is cozy – warm, dark, quiet, soft, liquid and all embracing. Suddenly, after some brutal squeezing, all of that comforting environment vanishes. Now there is bright light, noise, hard surfaces, loss of body contact and this strange sensation of being surrounded, not by liquid, but by air. No wonder the baby lets out a cry of panic.

new surroundings

The environment into which a baby is born is traditionally one of hospital efficiency, where it is deemed imperative for the procedure to be swift and hygienic. As rapidly as possible, the medical team cut and clamp the umbilical cord and examine the baby for defects. They then weigh him, wash him and wrap him in a snug blanket. For the vast majority of babies, who are born fit and healthy, the mood could easily be more relaxed and calm and this would lessen the shock of birth.

gently does it

Observations of newborn babies reveal that they are far less traumatized by the drama of being born if they are greeted, not by noise and excitement, but by peace and quiet, and in a room with soft lighting. Bright light may be needed for the birth itself, but once the baby has arrived safely, dimming the lights allows his eyes to adapt more gradually to the new demands put upon them.

Allowing a newborn baby to remain in close contact with his mother's body, instead of being picked up and examined right away by other hands, also greatly reduces his sense of panic at the loss of soft body contact. Placed on his mother's stomach so that she herself can embrace him, a baby will sense a continuity of the warm body intimacy he has been enjoying for the past nine months. It is no accident that the umbilical cord is of just the right length – approximately 20 inches (50 cm) – to make this possible while the baby is still attached to the placenta.

Babies treated in this more relaxed way demonstrate far less panic. There is no prolonged screaming or grimacing. The infant lies quietly on his mother's body, as he slowly recovers from his difficult journey. As far as the baby is concerned, there is no urgency at this point. His cord is still active and continues to beat for several minutes after the delivery is complete. During this time he starts to breathe the air, with his little lungs slowly taking over from the activity of the cord. This switch, if not interfered with, is a gradual one. At the same time, he receives the last drop of blood available to him from the cord supply.

early intimacy

Those assisting at the birth are probably impatient to get a baby washed, weighed and wrapped up but, if they wait a little while, both mother and baby will have time to experience the first sensations of bonding. The baby soon succumbs to the deep sleep of recovery, but for a while immediately after birth he is wide awake and, if allowed to do so, spends a great deal of time staring up at his mother as she looks down at him. In an ideal world, neither should be robbed of these intimate moments.

Eventually, the time comes for the baby's cord to be cut, and for him to be taken away for cleaning, weighing and wrapping up. If he has experienced this quiet time in his mother's arms he finds this interruption far less stressful. Once clean, a baby should be returned to his mother's arms and the two should be separated as little as possible during the first few days of his new life.

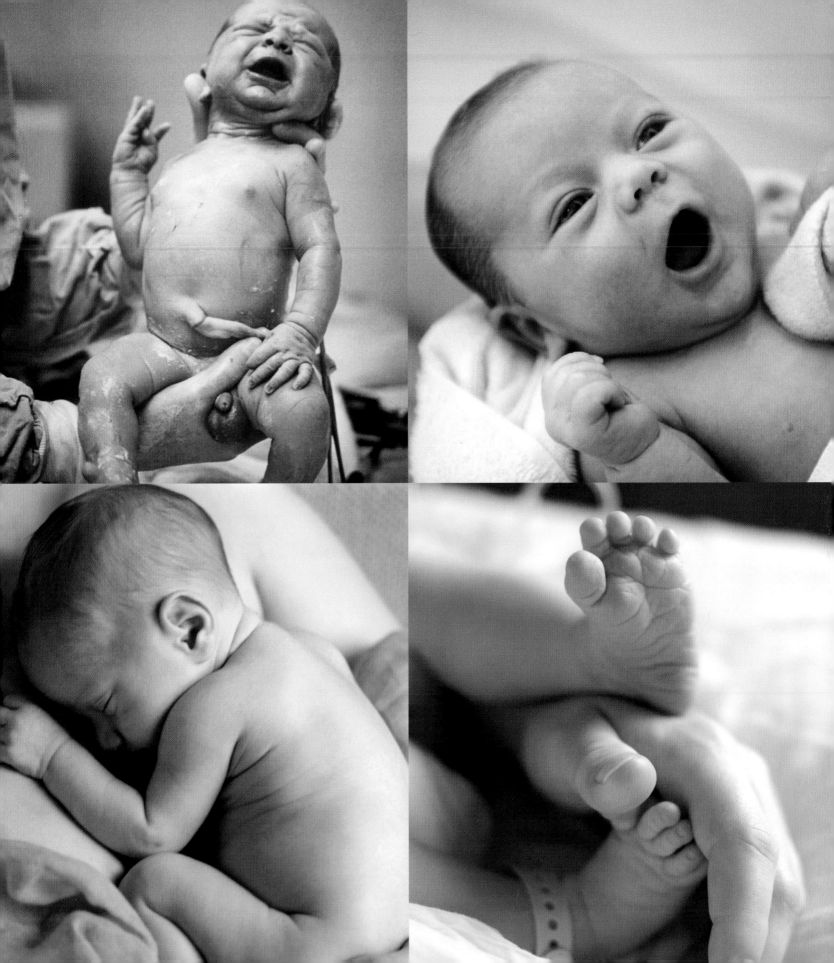

the newborn body

During her first few days of life outside the womb, a baby's body may seem less than perfect, but the early blemishes soon disappear. She has, after all, been lying curled up inside the womb for months and has just undergone the physical trauma of being squeezed, with some difficulty, through the birth canal: it is not surprising that she shows a few signs of these past experiences in her first days of freedom.

initial imperfections

A newborn baby's skin may show signs of her recent ordeal. These include red marks on the head and neck, sometimes referred to as "stork bites," which are tiny blood vessels visible through the skin. There may also be spots, rashes and peeling skin. All of these marks start to disappear as the body recovers from the rough treatment of being born and the baby adapts to life outside the womb. In the immediate period after birth, parents may see what is known as the "harlequin" effect. One half of the baby's body turns a deep red, while the other remains pale. This harmless reaction is caused by variations in the diameter of the blood vessels and is usually triggered by a change in position or temperature. Mottling of the skin is also common, owing to the immaturity of the circulatory system.

Eyelids may be puffy from the pressure exerted on them during birth but these, too, soon recover. Sometimes a baby may appear to have a squint during her earliest weeks, but this nearly always disappears during the first few months.

As she does not have to squeeze through the narrow birth canal, a baby arriving by cesarean delivery will be unblemished and her skull will not be distorted. However, a cesarean is a major operation – not without risk to mother and baby – and should only be performed for medical reasons. Research has shown that cesarean babies are more likely to have breathing difficulties, as it is thought they may miss out on important hormonal and physiological changes that occur during labor.

belly button

Shortly after birth the umbilical cord is clamped and cut, close to the navel. The piece that remains attached to the baby's belly soon starts to dry up naturally. This happens much faster if the stump is exposed to the air. Once dry and withered, the clamp is removed and the remaining piece of cord drops off of its own accord, usually within about 10 days, leaving behind a clean navel, or "belly button." It may take a little longer – anything up to three weeks – before it detaches itself, but it is important to let nature take its course. When it does finally happen there may be a few drops of blood, but these soon dry up. The resulting belly button may be convex (an "outie") or concave (an "innie") – both are completely normal.

breasts and genitals

In four or five out of every 100 newborn babies, there is a discharge of milk from the nipples. This is caused by the stimulation of the baby's breasts by unusually high levels of

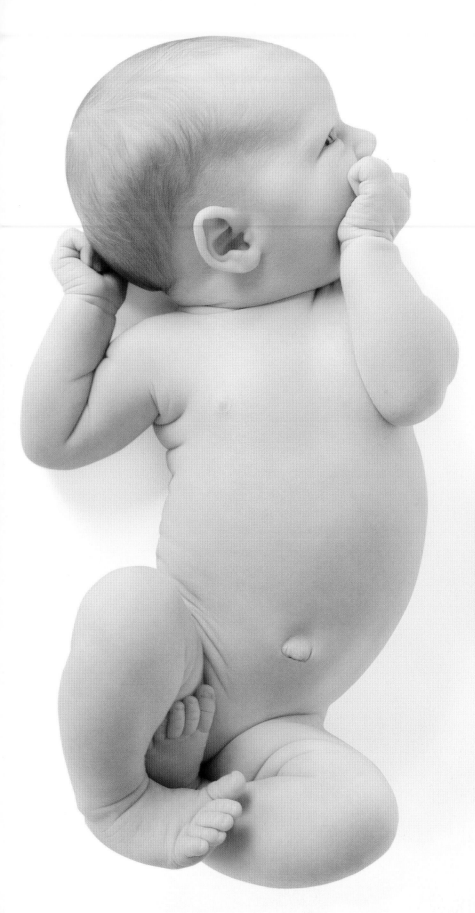

the mother's hormones that leak across the placenta during pregnancy and remain in the baby's system during her earliest days following birth. This discharge of milk is never seen in premature babies, only in those that reach full term. When it occurs, there is a small swelling, or breast nodule, underneath the nipple. Best left untouched, this may appear in both girl and boy babies and disappears within a few weeks.

Again, because of the presence of the mother's hormones in the new baby's system for the first few weeks of life outside the womb, it is perfectly natural for both boys and girls to be born with disproportionately large genitals. This is especially true of the male scrotum.

body shape

At birth, a baby's arms and legs are unusually short. Her length, relative to the rest of the body, continues to increase until she is fully adult. A newborn baby's shoulders and hips are rather narrow. The head is proportionally huge, being one-quarter of the total body length, compared to only one-eighth of the total adult length. During the first week or so, instead of growing, a baby's weight may actually decrease by about 5 percent, but this is perfectly normal and is due to a reduced intake of fluids: it takes a while for the mother's milk to come in and the baby feeds on the more concentrated colostrum for the first few days. She returns to her birth weight within 10 to 20 days and shows a steady increase from then on.

a baby's head

At birth, a baby's head creates a problem for his mother. When prehistoric woman first stood up on hind legs and started to walk, her pelvis had to adapt to this new mode of vertical locomotion. This meant a more restricted birth canal and a more difficult delivery. If the fetal skull were broad and stiff, a baby's passage into the outside world would be too clumsy and painful. There needed to be, therefore, some kind of streamlining in order to ease a baby's headfirst journey from the womb.

a modified skull

At the time of his birth, a baby's skull is amazingly soft and pliable. Although later on it must act as a rigid, biological crash helmet, protecting the all-important brain, at this stage it is more concerned with the challenge of being squeezed through the mother's vaginal passage. The softness of the bones helps, but there is more. In addition to their pliability, these skull bones are divided up into a number of separate plates, each capable of overlapping slightly with others. This gives the baby's head a slimmer, more tapered shape as it passes down the tight birth canal. The baby's small, movable jaw aids this process further.

natural distortions

The wonderful flexibility of a newborn's skull can leave a baby looking a little battered, even lopsided, as he emerges into the outside world. These distortions are a natural part of the birth process and soon disappear. Within a few days, almost every baby has a perfectly shaped and symmetrical skull, the soft bony plates having gradually rearranged themselves. Even in the most extreme cases, where the delivery has been unusually difficult, the remolding of the baby's skull takes no more than a few weeks. This skull distortion is most conspicuous with first-time mothers. The passage through the canal becomes easier with each subsequent birth until, eventually, there is hardly any distortion at all.

Following birth, a baby's skull takes several months to harden and become the efficient, protective casing that his brain so badly needs. During this early phase, it is especially vulnerable to physical damage and the mother has to be careful to offer as much protection as she can.

soft spots

The bony plates of a baby's skull remain separate for a time after birth. Small gaps between them are covered by a tough, membranous tissue that is strong enough to resist all forms of damage except a sharp, direct blow. At six points on the head, however, these narrow gaps widen out to form "soft spots" called fontanelles.

The two main fontanelles are on top of the head. The anterior fontanelle is located at the top of the forehead; the posterior one is toward the back of the top of the head. The four remaining, minor, soft spots are paired. The front pair is situated on either side of the temples; the rear pair is on either side toward the back of the head. It is sometimes possible to see a baby's pulse beating through the main anterior fontanelle.

These soft spots gradually disappear as the bony plates spread outward toward one another. The plates eventually touch, forming wavy sutures where they meet. These connections become harder and stronger until the whole skull is welded together and the infant's "crash helmet" has been perfected. The time this takes varies from child to child, the quickest time being about four months; the longest about four years. In most cases, however, completion takes between 18 and 24 months.

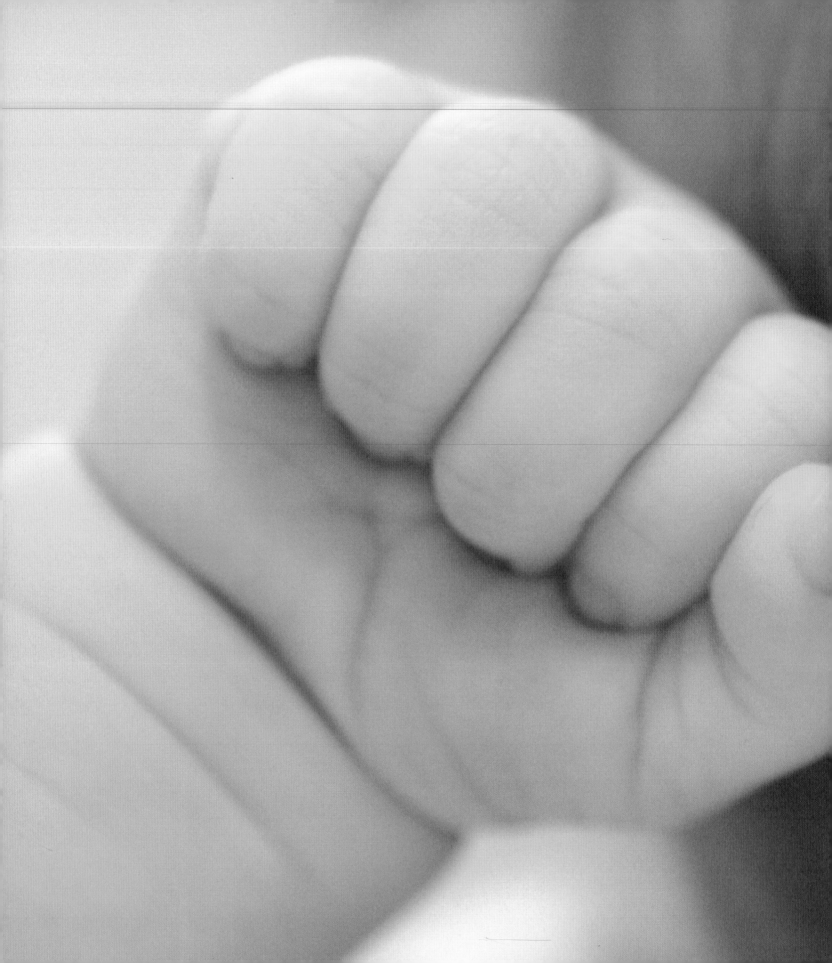

how a baby grows

gestation

Most mammals give birth to a litter of babies, but the human mother typically gestates only one offspring at a time. If her reproductive life continues unhindered, however, she finds herself gestating her second baby while her first is still very young and vulnerable. In this way she may produce a "serial litter" of infants of different ages, all requiring her attention. So, although multiple births may be a rarity for the human mother, she is nevertheless faced with the possibility of caring for a large and very demanding family.

the period of gestation

It is well known that, in human beings, the period between conception and birth lasts for nine months, but this is only a rough guide. Length of gestation varies considerably from woman to woman and a healthy baby may be born anywhere between 240 and 293 days (34 and 42 weeks) after the egg has been fertilized. If born after a pregnancy of fewer than 240 days (34 weeks), a baby is classified as "premature"; if born after more than 293 days (42 weeks) she is said to be "overdue." The most likely length of time between conception and birth is 266 days (38 weeks), or, for those trying to guess the day of the happy event, 280 days (40 weeks) after the last menstrual period (LMP).

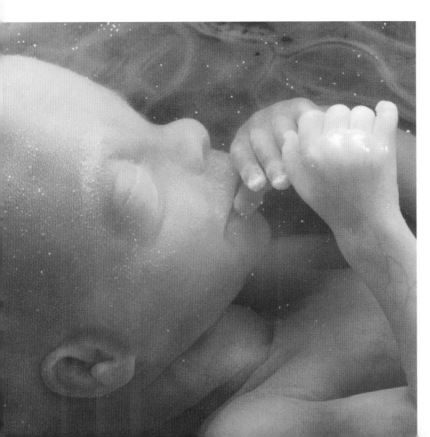

variations

One strange fact about the gestation period is that a female fetus seems to be more reluctant to leave the snug warmth of her mother's womb than her male counterpart. On average, female babies spend a day longer in the womb than male babies. There are also some racial differences. White babies, on average, spend five days longer inside their mothers than black babies, while Indian babies spend six days longer in the womb than white babies. It has been suggested that these geographical differences may have something to do with the size of the babies or the affluence of the mothers, but this is not the case. The variations are purely racial, but nobody knows why they should exist.

optimum conditions

The very best chance a baby has of surviving gestation is when her mother is aged 22. This has been described as "the age of fecundity" in humans, when fetal deaths are at their lowest level – just 12 out of every 1,000. Chances of a trouble-free birth are also extremely good for mothers who are anywhere between the ages of 18 and 30. Older mothers run a slightly increased risk, but even at the age of 45, fetal deaths are still only at the level of 47 in every 1,000. A few women have even managed to give birth in their 50s, although this is extremely rare because the average age for menopause is 51.

growth in the womb

The baby inside the womb grows at an astonishing rate, but his rapidly changing shape is hidden from us. All we can see is the swelling abdomen of the mother as the time of birth approaches. Thanks to modern technology, however, we do now know a great deal about each phase of the gestational period, from fertilization to birth.

first month

When the egg is fertilized by the sperm it forms a zygote. This divides into a number of cells and eventually becomes hollow, when it is referred to as the blastocyst. This moves down the fallopian tube and becomes attached to the lining of the mother's uterus, a process called implantation. In rare cases, the blastocyst separates into two units, creating what become identical twins. This happens between days five and nine. If it happens later than day nine there is a high risk of conjoined, or Siamese, twins being formed.

Some of the outer cells of the developing embryo become embedded deeply in the lining of the mother's uterus and it is these that eventually become the placenta. Once the dividing cells begin to differentiate, a groove forms that eventually becomes the spinal cord. By the age of three weeks the embryo has grown to a length of ⅛ inch (4 mm) and is already starting to curve into a C-shape. The heart bulge forms and begins to beat, arm buds are present and the embryo now has a tail. At four weeks the embryo has reached ¼ inch (8 mm) in length and the first signs of what will be major organs are beginning to differentiate. Eyes start to develop and nasal pits begin to form. Leg buds are now present and there are paddlelike hands at the ends of the arms.

second month

By the fifth week of growth the embryo measures ½ inch (13 mm) in length and the limbs become more clearly defined – the hands and feet even have digits. The brain is developing and the lungs begin to form. In the sixth week, the length increases to ¾ inch (18 mm) and all major organs have started to develop. Hair follicles, nipples and elbows start to form. Limb movements may already occur. Growth continues fast and in the seventh week the embryo

is 1¼ inches (3 cm) in length and the details of its face and head become more clearly defined, including the eyelids and the external ears. By the eighth week, the embryo has formed all its major organs and from now until birth it is referred to as the fetus. For the next seven months there will be continued growth and organ development, but all the basic structures are by now in place.

third month

The fetus is now 3¼ inches (8 cm) and is, for the first time, able to make a fist by clenching its fingers. Its limbs are longer, the liver is active, the genitals are differentiated and tooth buds begin to show. The fetus closes its eyelids at this stage and does not open them again until the seventh month.

fourth month

During this phase, the fetus doubles its length to 6 inches (15 cm). It performs active movements and its lips make sucking motions. It has hair on its head, the muscles and bones are stronger and the pancreas is active.

fifth month

The fetus is now 8 inches (20 cm) long and its whole body is covered by lanugo (see Newborn skin, page 18). Week 18 sees the appearance of eyelashes, eyebrows, fingernails and toenails. For the first time, the mother senses her baby moving inside her womb, a feeling that is known as the "quickening." It is always an exciting moment because it confirms that there is a real life inside.

sixth month

By the middle of this period the fetus reaches a length of 11 inches (28 cm) and weighs 1 pound 7 ounces (725 g). Footprints and fingerprints are forming on the feet and hands, and the eyes are more fully developed. The lungs contain air sacs. If alarmed by a sudden stimulus, the fetus is capable at this stage of performing the startle reflex (see A baby's reflexes, page 24). Some mothers may not feel the first movements of the baby until the end of this period – the time range for experiencing the quickening varies between 18 and 24 weeks.

seventh month

At around 26 weeks, the fetus reaches 15 inches (38 cm) long and weighs 2½ pounds (1.2 kg). Its eyes are now opening and closing and it can hear noises, such as the sounds of its mother's bodily functions, including her heartbeat, and even sounds like loud music that come from outside the body. The brain, nervous system and respiratory system show rapidly increased development. Babies born prematurely at the end of this month may survive, but the risks are high.

eighth month

By the middle of this period the fetus has probably grown to a length of 17 inches (43 cm), although there is some variation. It weighs about 4 pounds 7 ounces (2 kg). The skeletal structure is fully developed but the bones are not yet hard. There is an increase in the amount of body fat. Babies born during this month are still premature, but the survival rate is slightly better.

ninth month

By the middle of this period the typical fetus is about 19 inches (48 cm) long and weighs up to 6 pounds 9 ounces (3 kg). Its body is getter fatter and it is losing its hairy lanugo coating. The fingernails are nearly full-grown. This is the earliest point at which a birth is not considered to be premature. The shortest gestation that is considered to be full term is 34 weeks (240 days).

10th month

By the middle of this period, the lanugo has gone, and the typical fetus is as much as 21 inches (53 cm) in length. This is the point at which birth is most likely – on the 266th day of gestation, or the 40th week since the last menstrual period (LMP). The amazing journey from fertilized egg to delivered baby is over.

race for life
Each ejaculation contains 400 million sperm. Thousands reach the egg, but usually only one penetrates the outer coat. When the nuclei of sperm and egg fuse, a zygote is formed.

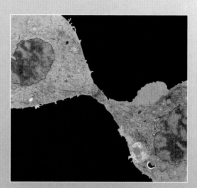

mitotic cell division
The cells of the growing baby multiply by mitosis, a process through which a cell doubles the number of chromosomes in its nucleus and splits into two new, identical daughter cells.

on the move

becoming mobile

Some young animals run around from the day they are born, but the human baby must wait several months before she can perform any kind of locomotion. Her body movements develop gradually and very slowly, in a predictable sequence.

first movements

The very first movements a baby makes are little more than gentle actions when exploring her mother's breast at feeding time. From these first clumsy touches she soon develops a variety of simple squeezing, grasping and rubbing motions as she investigates the surfaces around her. She soon learns to tell the difference between hard and soft, rough and smooth, cool and warm.

Although a baby may kick and wave her arms around if she attempts to move her whole body at this very early stage, her actions usually go no further than squirming or wriggling when she is uncomfortable or miserable. Her first real body movement comes when she discovers that, if she digs her heels in and kicks, she is thrust forward. Despite this small triumph, the first few weeks of a baby's life are truly helpless.

from chin-up to chest-up to bottom-up

Mobility slowly increases as the weeks pass. Placed on her front, a baby strains to lift her chin off the ground, as though she is not happy with this particular position. This first happens at about four weeks, although proper head control does not arrive for several months yet and her heavy head continues to need support when held. In her attempts to raise herself up, the head end of the baby is always slightly more advanced than the rear end.

At the age of about 16 weeks, a baby is capable of pushing upward with her arms and, a little later, manages to do the same with her legs. At first, however, she can only achieve these chest-up and bottom-up postures one at a time. It is as if she is preparing to crawl on her hands and feet by perfecting the two halves of the action separately, but she still cannot do both simultaneously. Perhaps in frustration, she may start to rotate on to her side at this point, finding that she can move herself around by rolling along.

from slither to crawl to walk

The next phase sees the development of the "slither" – a sort of commando crawl – in which a baby drags herself forward with her tummy on the ground, and uses both arms and legs to propel herself along. At seven months she at last finds that she can sit up unaided and control her sitting posture. Her body is stronger now and, at about eight months, the full crawl begins and the baby is, for the first time, truly mobile. This phase persists for several months until the baby struggles to adopt the vertical posture, first with parental help and then on her own. Once she can stand, walking is imminent and the baby becomes a toddler.

the muscles

Born with little muscular ability, the newborn baby has a greater degree of muscle control by 24 weeks of age. A parent can help by supporting the baby while he is sitting or standing, and watching as he makes an effort to maintain the position. He may not succeed but, in the process of trying, a baby learns something about his developing muscle systems by testing out the upper limits of his various body postures and movements.

muscle growth

A baby possesses all of his muscle fibers when he is born, although at this stage they are small and watery. As they grow, these neonatal fibers become longer, thicker and less watery. This development progresses in a "head to tail" sequence, with the muscles nearer the head end of the body always being slightly in advance of those to the rear. When a baby finally reaches adulthood, his muscles are 40 times as strong as they were at birth. Male babies have more muscle tissue than female babies, a difference that persists throughout life, and their physical growth is more variable than that of female babies.

types of muscle

Like an adult, a baby has three kinds of muscle. Striped, or striated, muscles are the voluntary muscles that operate the movements of the limbs, neck and face. They are all attached to the skeleton and are sometimes referred to as "skeletal muscles." As a baby grows, he develops more and more precise control over the actions of these muscles.

Smooth muscles are involuntary. There is no conscious control over them and their activities go unnoticed unless something is wrong. Smooth muscles control the movement of food through the intestines, the circular ones squeezing the gut and the longitudinal ones widening it. Smooth muscles also control the salivary glands, squeezing them during eating and moistening the food. The iris of the eye, changing with the intensity of the light, is also operated automatically by smooth muscles.

Cardiac muscles are striped, but are also involuntary. They automatically create a steady heartbeat, and one that can speed up or slow down according to the amount of physical activity taking place. They also speed up the heartbeat during moments of fear, anger or anxiety because these are moods that anticipate increased physical activity (which may or may not ultimately occur).

working in pairs

All three muscle types can contract themselves actively but can only expand passively. They must therefore work in opposing pairs, one of them forcibly contracting while its opposite number relaxes and allows itself to be stretched out. For example, if the biceps muscles in the arm contract, the arm bends. Then, if the triceps muscles contract, the arm straightens itself again. As the arm moves back and forth, there is no active muscle stretching, but simply two opposing contractions. The power of this system is weak in the newborn baby but slowly gathers strength as he grows.

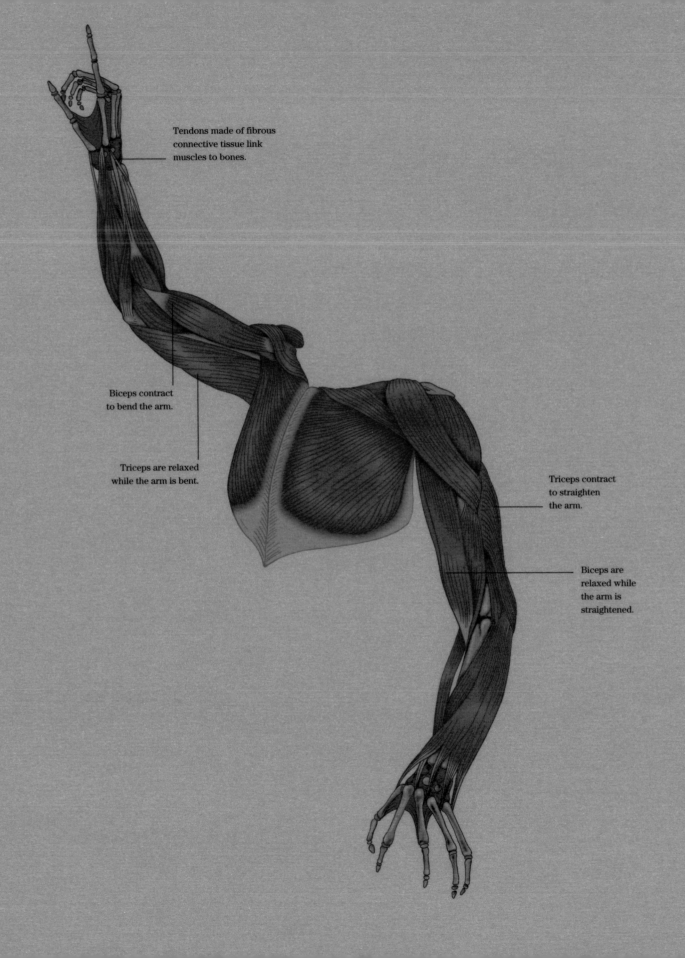

Tendons made of fibrous
connective tissue link
muscles to bones.

Biceps contract
to bend the arm.

Triceps are relaxed
while the arm is bent.

Triceps contract
to straighten
the arm.

Biceps are
relaxed while
the arm is
straightened.

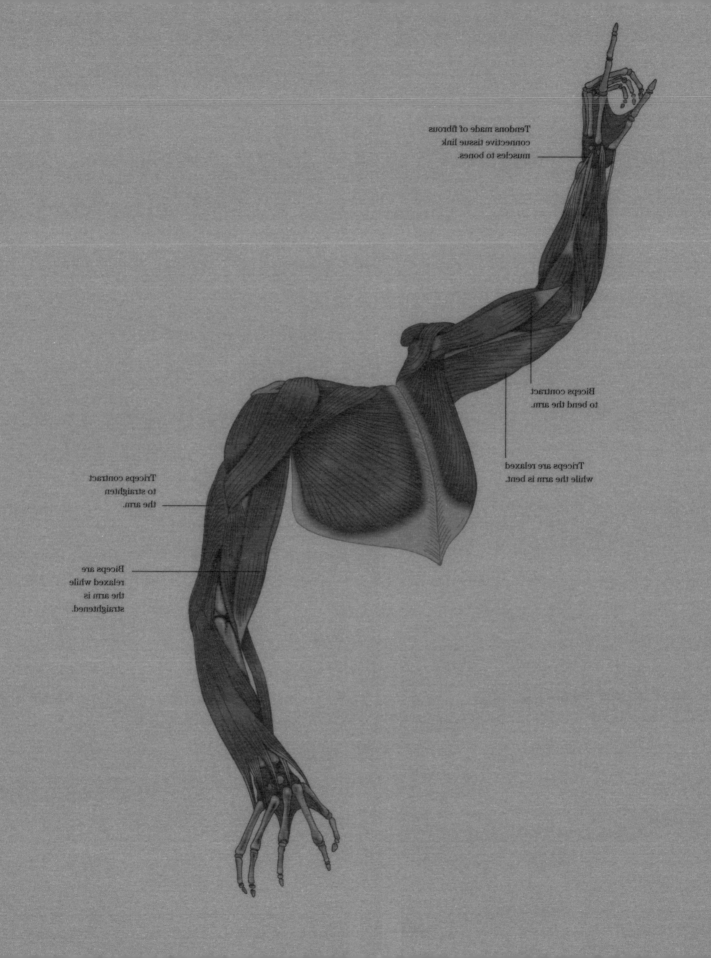

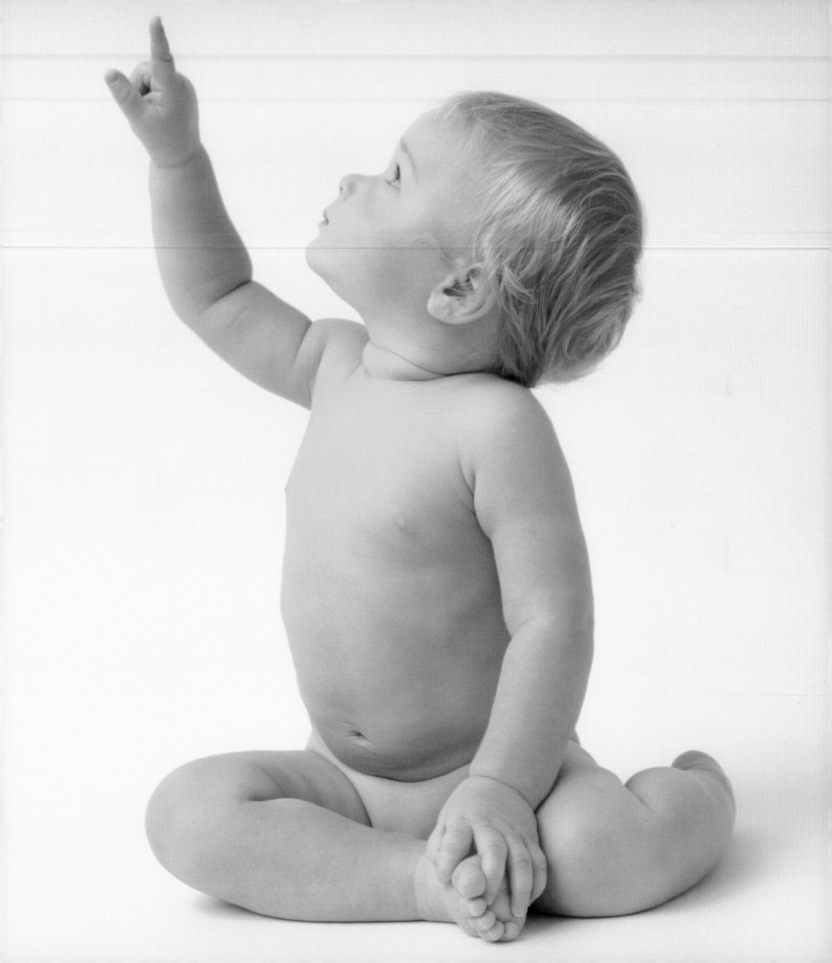

flexibility

During the early months, when her bones are still rather soft and bendable, a baby enjoys a remarkable degree of body flexibility. She can perform odd movements and adopt strange postures that only an adult contortionist could hope to achieve. She can, for example, grab her own toes and pull her foot toward her mouth.

Baby massage has become increasingly popular and it is claimed that, by giving your baby a gentle daily massage, you can increase her flexibility as well as improve her blood circulation, increase coordination and help the development of good posture. The truth is that the natural growth of a healthy infant should provide all the physical improvements that are necessary. As babies adore physical contact a daily massage can only do good, but it is unlikely to increase her natural flexibility. As the baby grows older, the very flexible, cartilaginous parts of her skeleton harden to bone and her infant flexibility is reduced as the body becomes stronger and increasingly mobile.

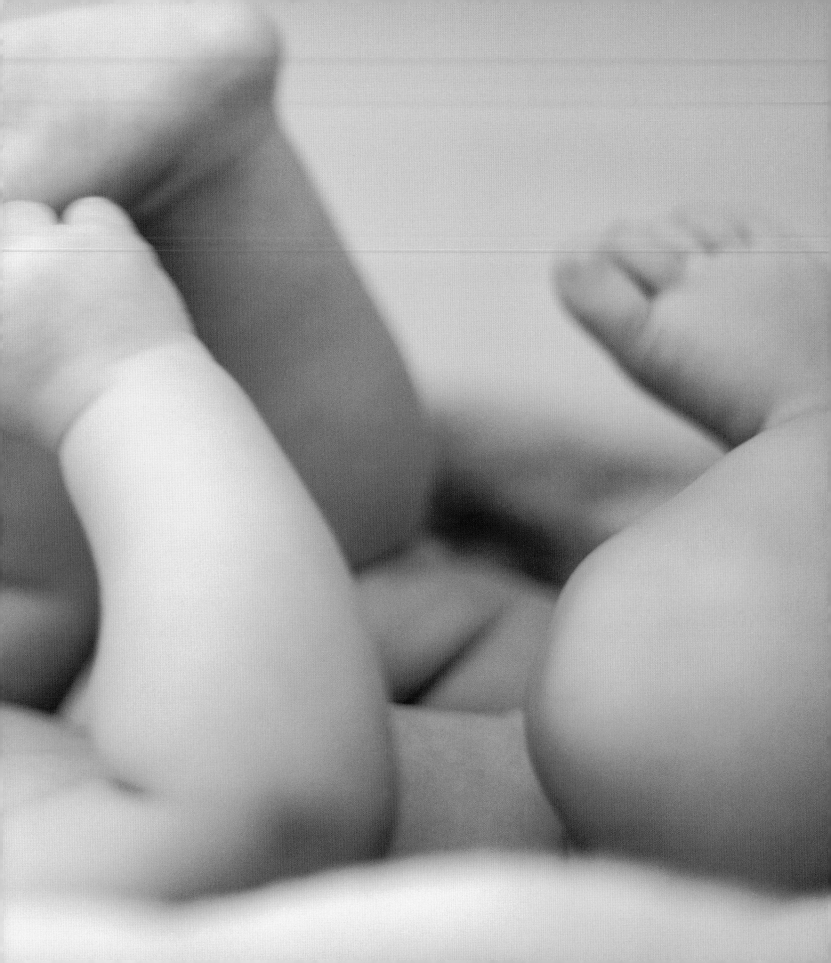

the hands

When a baby is born his small hands are incapable of precise movements. Apart from his powerful inborn grasp reflex (see A baby's reflexes, page 23), he does little with his fingers other than clench them tight. Soon, however, his hands are capable of reaching out and grasping hold of small objects that catch his attention. The next, vital stage is reaching out, grasping and then pulling the held object to the mouth for examination. Later on, his fingers are capable of more delicate, more precise actions in addition to the primitive power grasp.

early movement

For the first few weeks following birth a baby's hands stay clenched most of the time. Then, at about six weeks, he tries pulling at one hand with the other. At eight weeks, he starts to experiment with opening and closing his fingers, and if he has a hanging toy dangling above him, he hits out at it to make it move.

palmar grasp

When a baby is 12 weeks old, his hand movements are more controlled as he hits out at objects near to him. He plays more with his hands now, exploring them to find out how they work. At 16 weeks, he tries out two-handed grasping and gathering objects toward him. The baby's movements are still clumsy, grasping an object with his whole hand rather than just his fingers, but the range of hand actions is developing all the time. By 20 weeks, his grasp is stronger and more efficient. There is a tendency to bring objects up to the mouth and investigate them with the lips and tongue.

clasping and letting go

As a baby enters his seventh month, his hand actions are advanced enough for him to start playing with wooden blocks and other similar toys. He can also move a held object from one hand to the other and back again, and can let go of the object voluntarily. At eight months, he extends his hand-to-mouth actions to attempt self-feeding. When given a drink, he may clasp the mug with his hands, struggling to hold it up to his mouth by himself, usually with little success. This is the stage when dexterity advances by leaps and bounds.

pincer movement

By now a baby has discovered the fun of clapping his hands together and the first sign of individual finger action appears, usually pointing using just the forefinger. This heralds the use of individual fingers and the major step of employing the thumb-and-forefinger precision grip that enables a baby to pick up and hold small objects with some accuracy – a stage most commonly reached in the tenth month after birth.

By the end of his first year, a baby is able to turn the pages of a simple book, clasp objects firmly, use his pincerlike precision grip more and more skillfully, pile up toys and knock them down again, and feed himself with a spoon. During the second year of life, all these manual skills are refined and developed, with more and more accurate control appearing week by week.

baby fingerprints

Fingerprints appear on the hands of babies even before they are born. Somewhere between the third and the fifth month inside the womb, the tiny fingers of the fetus start to show patterns of ridges. These are unique to each individual and once formed will stay the same for the entire life span. Even though the fingerprints enlarge as the hands grow bigger, the complex patterns of ridges do not change.

hand activity

A baby goes through a complicated sequence of "hand phases" as she advances through the first few years of life. It is as if a pendulum swings back and forth from left to right, first favoring one hand and then the other. By the time the pendulum stops swinging the child settles on one hand and becomes either right- or left-handed for the rest of her life. But while it is swinging back and forth, matters are not at all clear about where it will finally stop.

early tendencies

If offered an object at three months, a baby usually holds out both hands at the same time. Arm movements are not at all precise and first one hand and then the other becomes dominant. At this early phase, therefore, there is no left or right bias. When offered an object at four months, a baby reaches out with one hand and, in the majority of cases, it is the left hand. Careful studies have revealed that the left bias at this phase of development has no bearing on adult hand preference. Indeed, this left bias disappears at six months and there is no strongly preferred hand.

pendulum swings

At around seven months the pendulum swings to the right. A baby still experiments, first with one hand and then with the other, but the overall bias is now toward right-handedness. The right bias disappears at eight months, however, and the baby uses left and right hands equally. The pendulum swings back to the left again at nine months, by which time the baby is more strongly left-handed than before. At 10 months there is yet another shift and the right hand once again becomes the dominant one.

At some time around 11 months, a baby may switch back to the left hand but, for the majority, it is still the right hand that dominates. This situation persists until the end of the first year of life and one might assume that handedness is now fixed for life. But this is not the case.

further experiments

Approaching 20 months confusion returns and a baby uses both hands again with no clear sign of hand bias. At the end of her second year, a baby's right hand regains the dominant role once more. Then, between the ages of two and a half and three and a half, a toddler goes through one last confused phase, with no particular hand dominating. After that, at about four years of age, the growing child at long last settles down to either a right or left bias. This preference grows stronger as the years pass and, by the time the child is eight years old, she arrives at her permanent handedness and is either right- or left-handed for the rest of her life.

left-handed or right-handed?

At this phase one child out of ten is left-handed and nine out of ten are right-handed. Nobody is certain why human beings have such a strong bias toward right-handedness. We do know from studies of ancient hand axes, however, that the bias has existed for at least 200,000 years, so it is not a modern development.

Some clues come from the way in which an unborn baby lies inside her mother's womb, when she establishes a preferred position toward the end of her pregnancy. The majority lie with their right sides closer to the mother's body surface. This may mean that the right side of the fetus receives more stimulation during pregnancy and becomes more advanced than the left. Anatomically, in the majority of cases, there are more nerves leading to the right side of the body of the fetus than to the left. And, at birth, a newborn baby shows stronger electrical activity on the side of the brain that controls the right side of the body. So it would seem that, from the very beginning, there is a slight bias toward the right.

a natural progression

The ability to walk survives the most restrictive regimes. Even in tribes and societies where infants are strapped to boards and carried by adults for long periods of time, the babies may reach their developmental milestones later than most children, but still eventually manage to walk, nevertheless. This shows that there is an amazing maturing process taking place in each baby that is programmed before birth.

six stages of walking

The very first signs that a baby is programmed for walking appear only a few days after birth. Supported by parental hands so that his feet just touch the ground, a newborn baby kicks out in a vigorous way as if trying to progress forward. These are automatic, reflex actions and cannot be controlled or modified by the baby (see A baby's reflexes, page 23). They disappear after about two months but are a clear indication that the action of bipedal walking is deeply embedded in the human brain.

stage two

This stage, from about two months, shows the growing baby quite incapable of performing any sort of prewalking actions. Held by parents now, with his feet just touching the ground, he simply sags at the knees. The early kicking actions have gone.

stage three

At about three months, or slightly later, instead of sagging at the knees when held over a hard surface, a baby's legs stiffen and attempt to support his body. As the weeks pass this "parentally supported" phase shows improvement, with the baby's legs becoming stronger and better able to keep his body erect.

stage four

Typically between six and nine months comes the "heaving upright" phase in which an active infant does his best to pull himself up on to his legs by grabbing hold of some convenient piece of furniture. Once he has managed this, he proudly surveys his new domain for a while and then promptly collapses with a bump, back down on to the ground. Unless he hits something on the way, this setback does not deter the baby for long. The sensation of being higher up in the world is irresistible and he soon heaves himself up once more, gradually becoming accustomed to the new sensation of supporting his body weight on his legs.

stage five

This stage is true forward walking with the aid of parental hands, and is usually first seen between the ages of nine and 12 months. It consists of a few faltering steps followed by a loss of balance. The parent prevents the baby falling over, but the baby finds these initial failures highly frustrating. He now knows exactly what he wants to do and is upset that he is too clumsy to achieve his goal. But he perseveres and each stumbling progression becomes a little more controlled than the last until the great moment arrives when he strides out alone to walk a few first unaided paces across the room.

stage six

A baby takes his first few tentative steps with arms held high and elbows bent as an aid to balance. The steps are wide apart, uneven in length and unsteady, but after a few months the movements are far more controlled and the arms are no longer held up for balance. By 18 months most toddlers are confident walkers and tumbles are rare.

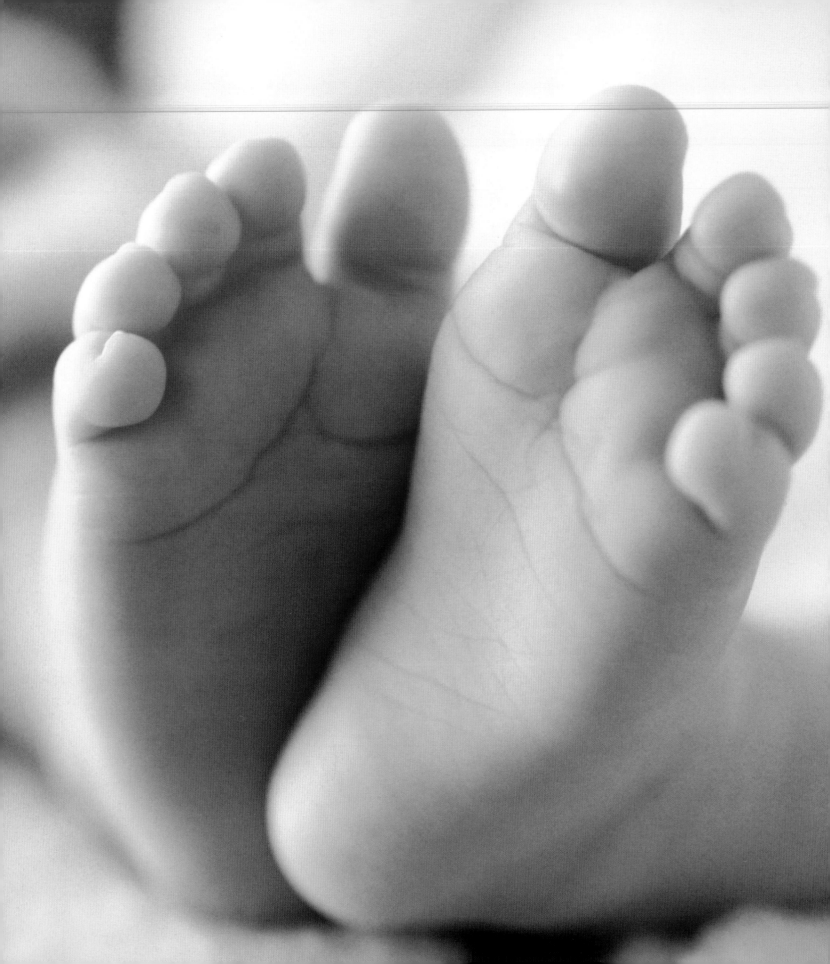

the feet

At birth, a newborn baby's feet are one-third of their adult length. At the age of one year they are nearly half their adult size. Apart from this size difference, a baby's feet differ from those of the adult in several ways. They are heavily padded with fat, making them much softer and rounder than adult feet. They are also much more flexible, as the bones inside them are still developing from cartilage to bone. And they tend to turn inward, giving the baby a pigeon-toed look. This last quality results from the fetus having been squashed up inside her mother's womb for so long before birth. By the time a baby is starting to walk, however, these newborn qualities are far less marked.

straight feet

The inward-turned feet of the newborn slowly straighten out as the months pass. Some parents are worried when they see their toddlers attempting to walk with a bandy-legged, pigeon-toed gait, but this is perfectly normal and is adjusted naturally as a child learns to walk less clumsily. There is no point in attempting to hurry the process.

baby shoes

Many years ago, parents were taught that, because toddlers had wobbly ankles and flat feet, they needed special shoes to help them walk. Stiff, high-top, hard-sole leather shoes were recommended to enable babies to walk sooner. However, modern research has found that toddlers are not, in fact, flat-footed. When played back in slow motion, video recordings of young children making their very first attempts at walking show that they use a heel-to-toe action similar to that seen in walking adults. Also, their ankles are capable of providing excellent balance. All that is needed when learning to walk, therefore, is a period of practice as the toddler learns how to perform this new kind of locomotion, and her foot muscles and ligaments toughen up from repeated use.

going barefoot

Studies of children growing up in shoeless, tribal cultures show that fewer foot problems are experienced than in countries where wearing shoes is the norm. The more a toddler is allowed to walk about with bare feet, the better the natural growth and development of her feet as the months pass. The barefoot toddler develops stronger and more coordinated muscles than the carefully shod one. Shoes should be worn, not for walking inside the family home, but for protection against harsh surfaces and against the elements when the infant is out and about.

climbing

Between the ages of seven and 12 months, a baby masters fast crawling sufficiently to want to explore new possibilities, and one activity that appeals is climbing. This proves an exhilarating experience, taking the infant literally to new heights (of which he seems fearless). The sudden arrival of more adventurous pursuits and investigations has its own hazards, however. The active baby may thrill to the novelty of unfamiliar experiences, but at the same time he is as unaware of what can go wrong, and therefore unprepared for any kind of danger.

allure of stairs

For some reason a stairway is a powerful draw for the fast-crawling baby. The hands-and-knees posture of the infant seems ideally suited to clambering up stairs at top speed. And the intrepid climber, never having fallen downstairs in his short life, is completely fearless as he ascends higher and higher. Now an awkward moment arrives. The baby, suddenly feeling that this particular climbing game is over, is faced with the problem of getting down again. Turning around and coming down headfirst is a dangerous option with the center of balance all wrong. Instead he needs the help of an adult in coming down backward.

standing and reaching up

For a baby of seven to 12 months, any object placed out of reach has a special attraction. If it is too high, he experiments with clambering up toward it, raising an arm as far as possible and then grabbing at it. This is often done clumsily, with the result that the object in question tumbles down on top of the baby. Curiosity knows no bounds at this stage, and it is remarkable just how many dangers there are lurking around an ordinary house, that can do harm to the more adventurous baby.

learning safely

For reckless babies, one solution is to install a baby gate to prevent access to the stairway. These work well at first, but can easily become a challenge for the baby – an obstacle to be overcome by risky clambering. A more drastic measure is the large playpen in which the demon crawler is confined and from which he has no escape. Stocked with soft toys, this will keep the crawler happy for a while and is useful as a brief resort when something urgent requires the attention of the mother, but eventually the confined space begins to frustrate the baby's inquisitive nature.

A baby thrives in a crawl-safe playroom, in which the entire area is hazard-free but offers plenty of room for him to exercise newfound skills. If he has a few small objects to climb over, placed on a soft carpet, he has the chance to experience the failure moment of falling without harming himself. He has to learn caution somehow and "safe accidents" are the only pleasant way to do this.

climbers and nonclimbers

Strangely, climbing does not have appeal for all infants. There is enormous variation in the juvenile urge to ascend. Some babies ignore high places altogether, some are mildly interested and others seem to be obsessed with them. The last group requires special watching. One father was startled to hear his toddler, not yet two years old, call out "Daddy" from just behind him. The reason this shocked him was because, at the time, he was repairing the roof of the family house. To his horror he realized that the infant had climbed up a tall ladder and was now perched on the roof behind him!

staying healthy

safe and well

A newborn baby has a degree of natural protection from the diseases that lurk in the outside world. In addition to a limited built in immune mechanism, he also acquires immunity from his mother's blood while he is in the womb. If he is breast-fed, he gains further immunity from his mother's milk, which is rich in antibodies. This is especially true during the first few days of his life in the outside world, when he receives the premilk, or colostrum.

Unfortunately this maternal protection does not last forever, but merely serves as an emergency defense during the earliest months, when the baby has not yet had the chance to obtain immunity in any other way. From this time on, his immune system develops defenses of its own through exposure to mild infections, which helps create the antibodies that protect him when something worse comes along (see A baby's defense system, page 96).

vaccination
In addition to a baby's developing immune system, there are a number of protective vaccinations that can help the infant to resist diseases that pose a particular threat. A baby usually makes five or six vaccination visits to the doctor during the first two years of life. It is true that some babies suffer minor side effects from vaccination, such as a mild fever, but it is generally recognized that the benefits of immunization easily outweigh the risks.

A vaccine is prepared by weakening or killing the disease-causing bacteria or viruses and then introducing them, by mouth or injection, into a baby's body. There they act as if they are the real disease and cause the defense system to produce protective antibodies. But they do this without causing the dangerous illness that usually goes with the disease if caught in the normal way. Once the baby produces the antibodies, these provide immunity for a long time.

multi-vaccines
Recently there has been some argument about the safety of new multi-vaccinations in which an infant is given five different disease protections with a single injection. This five-in-one immunization is given at eight, 12 and 16 weeks of age, and protects the baby against diphtheria, tetanus, whooping cough, *Haemophilus influenzae* type B (Hib) and polio. Critics of this procedure claim that there is a danger of overloading the baby's immune system, but medical authorities insist that a large number of clinical trials show that there is little or no risk of this. In addition to the five-in-one jab, it is also possible to provide protection against various other diseases, such as hepatitis B, with an injection given shortly after the birth of the baby, and measles, mumps and rubella (MMR), given later, at the age of 12 to 15 months.

parental protection
The human infant is remarkably resilient, heals quickly and has a good immune system but, despite this, he takes a long time to develop either the sensitivity or the necessary motor skills to keep him safe within his environment. Modern cities and buildings are full of dangers that did not exist in prehistoric times, such as the many toxic household products, and infants have no natural reactions to protect them from such artificial hazards.

A baby must learn to avoid injury by experience, therefore minor bumps and bruises may cause frantic crying but in the long run they become part of the learning process by which a growing child acquires a greater dexterity and "native cunning" in dealing with the hazards of his environment. The trick is for the parent to find as many ways as possible of reducing the dangers present in an otherwise rich environment, so that the infant can enjoy full expression with the minimum of risk.

development of speech

While a baby's urge to babble and gurgle in the earliest months is inborn, his later urge
to develop this babbling into spoken language is learned by attentive imitation. A baby
who instinctively makes single-syllable vowel sounds at the age of three months starts,
voluntarily, to make a number of two-syllable sounds at seven months and begins to learn
words from eight months. By 10 months, he utters his first word and he has three words
by the end of his first year.

vocabulary building

The pace at which a baby's language skills develop is
truly astounding. A child that has as many as 19 words
by the time he reaches 15 months has some 200 to 300
by the end of his second year and can make rudimentary
sentences using verbs, pronouns and plurals. As always,
there is considerable variation from infant to infant. For
example, one survey of a group of children aged 20 months
revealed that a number already had a 350-word vocabulary,
while others had learned only six words.

baby talk

Many parents adopt a high-pitched goo-goo kind of baby
talk when conversing with their infants. Referred to as
"parentese," it involves talking in a sing-song kind of way,
typically elongating vowel sounds and making exaggerated
facial expressions. Sentences are short and parents tend to
talk slowly and deliberately, often repeating a phrase over
and over again. All adults do this, throughout the world and
regardless of their age or relationship to a baby.

While parentese is beneficial to a young baby, helping him
to recognize familiar sounds and words, it is no longer
particularly helpful by the time the baby approaches the
end of his first year. At this stage the growing infant needs
to imitate his parents. If the opposite is happening the
learning process is curtailed. Instead, parents who speak
to a child in normal adult voices provide the little ones
with a much richer, more stimulating variety of sounds
and inflections to imitate.

origins of speech

A baby seems to be capable, even in the earliest month of
life, of making several different and quite distinct types of
"grunt" revealing his mood. One kind of grunt indicates
discomfort, for example, another tiredness, another hunger
and another gas. It has been pointed out that these grunts,
as well as the baby's first attempts to create simple words
such as "mama" and "dada," are much the same the world
over (see The arrival of speech, page 110). It has therefore
been suggested that these utterances, common to all
humanity, probably represent the kind of primeval language
first used by our ancient ancestors, before humans started
splitting into groups and developing different kinds of adult
language.

Recordings of baby gurglings reveal that there are four
sequences of sound patterns, each consisting of a particular
consonant-vowel combination, and that these are common
to cultures with adult languages as different as Swedish,
Portuguese, Korean, Japanese, French and Dutch. There
was probably a time when our evolving ancestors could
manage little more than these few utterances. The next
step would have been to repeat these primitive sounds in a
rhythmic manner – "babababababa" or "gagagagagaga" – to
make longer units, and this process is still very common
today in the earliest attempts of babies to make words.
Learning adult speech is an extremely complex procedure
involving the coordination of no fewer than 70 different
muscles, and babies have to be patient while slowly gaining
full control of these muscles.

listening and babbling

Vocal communication involves two distinct elements – listening to sounds and making them. A baby is always slightly more advanced as a listener than as a sound-maker. She is even able to hear words when she is still inside the womb. This means that she is responsive to parental voices from the day she is born, even though it is several months before she herself starts to make babbling sounds.

babies and listening

When the fetus is six or seven months old, she is already capable of hearing sounds made in the outside world. Tests have shown that a baby's heart rate dips slightly on hearing a new, loud noise. At each repeat of the sound, the baby's reaction lessens until, eventually, there is no observable dip. The baby has become conditioned to that particular sound. If a new sound is now introduced, the dip in heart rate immediately reappears, proving that the fetus can distinguish between one sound and another. Further tests have demonstrated that an unborn fetus is capable of distinguishing between two very similar words and that her listening ability is clearly far in advance of her speaking.

What this demonstrates is that, by the time she is born, a baby has already come to know her mother's voice and can distinguish it from all other voices. Similar experiments with music reveal that a fetus is capable of telling one kind of music from another, and is even able to tell one nursery rhyme from another. There is, of course, no suggestion that she can understand the content of musical compositions or rhymes. What she is detecting is no more than different sound patterns, but even that is extraordinary enough and explains why very young babies are so fascinated by making a variety of simple sounds themselves, as soon as they discover how.

the bubbling phase

The stream of sounds made by a young baby passes through a number of phases during her first year of life, after which it is replaced by the serious business of forming words. When only one or two months old, a baby discovers that she can perform a bubbling action by pushing her tongue out through her slightly parted lips and then closing the lips again. A little bubble of saliva emerges from her mouth. As yet, no sound accompanies this great achievement, but it is the very first step on the long road to verbal fluency. In making this prebabbling action, the baby is mouthing the actions of vocalizing, coordinating her breathing with the movements of the tongue and lips. It is this vital combination that later provides the basis for true speech.

the cooing phase

At the age of three months, audible babbling arrives on the scene. As the weeks pass, this new discovery – the ability to make noises – fascinates a baby more and more, and babbling becomes an obsession. At first there is little more than splutters and grunts and rude noises, but then the first open vowel sounds are made. Now the baby experiments with ooooos and aaaaas, and parents find it hard not to join in with cooo-cooos and gooo-goooos.

the advanced babbling phase

The babbling reaches a crescendo at the age of six months. It is such fun that a baby often happily burbles away when she is completely alone. Consonants now join the vowels to produce a wide variety of single-syllable sounds. But there is still no relationship between these sounds and any specific object or person. They are "sounds for sound's sake" without any reference or specific meaning – like a singer practicing the scales without making a song.

first words

The first word with specific meaning uttered by an infant is usually "mama" or "dada," and is directed at parents as they chatter to their offspring. It is a moment of great joy, and parents are usually keen to demonstrate the passing of this important threshold to their friends. Unfortunately, when the infant sees an old friend of his father's peering down at him, he is liable to call him "dada" as well.

This is merely a reflection of the fact that, as yet, the infant is only just beginning to put word to person. Mother may also be called "dada," and father "mama," but little by little the links between specific sounds and specific individuals are established. It is this stage that is the true passing of a major threshold.

the preverbal phase

Before words are spoken with a specific meaning, however, there is one final phase of undirected sound-making. This arrives at about seven months and consists of making two-syllable words. Usually the first syllable is the same as the second one, as with "mumum," "dadad" or "booboo." The baby is now exploring, not only more complicated double sounds, but also trying out variations in volume, pitch and speed. He is like a tiny orchestra tuning up before a great concert performance. He cannot play the music yet, but he can at least test out his instruments. His utterances may occasionally sound like true words, but as yet they have no real meaning. The next phase – and the thrill of being able to communicate with his parents – is almost upon him, but not quite. When this stage does finally arrive, it soon sweeps the joys of babbling into the past and replaces them with the more serious business of starting to learn a functional vocabulary.

tone of voice

Vocal communication is more than a verbal exchange. It also involves tonality. A baby is sensitive to two contrasting types of "tone of voice" – smooth and harsh – and he also distinguishes between soft and loud. He dislikes harsh or very loud voices, even when the spoken words are identical to those uttered by smooth, soft voices. If an adult coos "I love you" to a baby, using a warm, gentle, loving tone, he enjoys the words. But if the same adult yells "I love you" using a harsh tone, the baby reacts unhappily. So, as the baby starts to acquire a vocabulary, it is important to remember that each word carries a tonal "modifier" that can dramatically change its significance.

early vocabulary

Once true words with specific meanings are uttered by a baby, it is fascinating to see which ones come first. They are nearly always one- or two-syllable words. Longer words defeat a baby in the earliest phase of speaking. He also ignores short words that relate to anything abstract or intangible. The very first "sentences" usually consist of no more than a noun, and the nouns are always someone or something that is visible at the time. The most popular first words with a meaning are dada, mama, grandma, grandpa, nose, mouth, doggy, kitty, ball, eat and drink, along with the nicknames of brothers, sisters and other family members. As the number of such verbal labels starts to grow, simple verbs are added, creating two-word sentences. As before, the baby's understanding of language is more advanced than his ability to speak it. If the mother asks "Where has kitty gone?", the baby looks around trying to locate the kitten, even though he may not yet be able to say the four-word sentence himself. Baby utterances are always trying to catch up with baby understanding, and it is this race that helps to drive the infant forward to ever better communication skills.

complex toys

A toddler often makes his own decisions as to what kind of toy excites him most. Tales abound of the child who is less interested in the expensive train set than in the box in which it came. This is because, unfortunately, many toys are designed with the parent in mind and not the child, so that some of the most elaborate toys also happen to be the least used. There are some exceptions to this general rule, however.

challenge toys

A toy that challenges a child's intelligence can quickly become a favorite, as long as it gives the infant a reasonable chance of success. If the child always solves a problem quickly, or never manages to do so at all, the toy is a failure. But if the child frequently gets it wrong, but sometimes gets it right, he is likely to return to the toy time and time again, drawn by the "occasional reward" factor. For a young baby, piling up blocks to make a tower that eventually falls over (or that he knocks down for fun), is a classic example of a challenging toy. It is not a simple matter of win or lose, but of how many bricks the baby can stack before the tower collapses. More advanced toys of this type appeal as the child grows older.

wheeled toys

One step up from simple building blocks is the four-wheel push-along wagon in which a one-year-old can place the blocks. He puts them in, pushes them to a new place, takes them out, builds them up, puts them back in again, moves to a new location, and so on. This involves standing upright with the support of the wagon handle. While concentrating on pushing, the child inadvertently familiarizes himself with the actions of walking. From here on, mobility increasingly becomes something of an obsession and a baby thrills at exploring the world on ride-along toys such as tricycles and pedal cars.

shape and construction toys

Simple shape-sorters appeal from 12 months, when a toddler readily accepts the challenge of fitting different shapes into holes. The excitement of making a star-shaped brick fit neatly into the star-shaped hole preoccupies him as an enjoyable game while at the same time teaching him a great deal about the geometry of familiar objects. Very simple jigsaw puzzles also offer a challenge, improving a toddler's familiarity with irregular shapes.

Toys made of several pieces that a toddler has to fit together in a certain way to create a whole are more complicated than earlier toys, and introduce the concept of "assembling." They test a toddler's visual awareness as well as hand-eye coordination, which becomes more refined as the months pass and the toddler learns to dress and undress a doll or assemble mechanical devices.

making music

Simple musical instruments that a toddler can hit or press to create a variety of notes also have appeal, the child reveling in the fact that something he does results in a funny noise or tuneful sound. A toddler may be shocked by a jack-in-the-box that springs up toward him after playing a tune, but once he recognizes the shock as a "safe" one (see Humor, page 154), he enjoys the experience again and again.

self-awareness

During her first year, a baby lacks any self-awareness. She is so engrossed in the discoveries she is making about the world around her that she pays little attention to herself. All of this changes during her second year, when she gradually becomes aware of her own identity.

the mirror test

When a tiny baby, just a few months old, is shown her reflection in a mirror it does not seem to occur to her that she is looking at a reflection of herself. She reacts to the mirror as just another toy – an exciting one because, as it moves around, its appearance changes. But she has no idea that she is looking at her own image. A fish or a bird reacts in the same way. If a mirror is placed on the animal's territory, it may attack the image, assuming that it is an intruder. Or, if it is in a mating mood, it may try to make sexual advances toward its own image.

When a toddler reaches the age of about 15 months, a moment of truth arrives. She looks in the mirror, waves her hand and the "other person" waves back in exactly the same way. She tries other actions and each is copied precisely. Eventually the child realizes that what she sees is really herself and not another child. A simple test can prove this, in which an infant is shown her face in a large mirror. She is then taken away and a hat is placed on her head, or a small mark made on her face with some makeup. Seeing her reflection again, she reacts in one of two ways. If she reaches out to touch the hat or the makeup mark on her reflection she has failed the test. If, however, she gazes in the mirror, sums up the situation and then reaches up to touch the real hat on her own head, or the real mark on her own face, she has passed the test, because she has proved that she recognizes the mirror image as her own face. By the age of about 18 months, half of all children tested in this way manage to pass the test. By the age of 24 months this figure rises to three-quarters of all children. And in the third year the remaining 25 percent also pass. To adults this seems such a ridiculously easy test and yet very few animals are capable of passing it. Apart from human toddlers, only chimpanzees, orangutans, dolphins, elephants and just one gorilla have managed it with any certainty.

a growing sense of "self"

This self-discovery and the understanding that she is a separate entity – a small person with her own independent existence – grows stronger as the second birthday approaches and goes a long way to explain the phenomenon known as "the terrible twos" (see A busy age, page 177). At this age, a child, having made the discovery that she is a complete being, like the ones she sees around her, is liable to become rather self-centered and often stubborn. She wants to do things *her* way and may get angry if she is not able to. Controlling her sometimes becomes a battle of wills, and parents need to adopt new strategies to deal with this obstinate phase.

separation anxiety

A toddler has a deep-seated fear of losing touch with his parental protectors. When very young, he may go into a state of screaming panic if he cannot locate his mother or father, or whoever has the role of principal caregiver. As time passes, however, he eventually learns that, in certain specific circumstances like being put to bed, he has to accept the departure of the loved ones, and there is nothing he can do about it. At these moments, he seeks out some form of substitute for the missing caregivers – a "transitional comfort object."

transitional comfort objects

Because the departing mother has a soft, cuddly body, the best substitute for her is something that is soft, smooth and warm to the touch and that the child can press against his cheek and hold tightly in his arms. For many children this means a piece of bedding, such as a blanket, which the child grabs, bunches up and holds to the side of his head. A toddler often falls asleep in this position, with his cheek pressed against the substitute mother's body. This then becomes a favorite object and something for the child to carry around for emergency use whenever he feels a pang of insecurity.

soft toys

A child who has a number of soft toys to play with during the day often selects just one of these as the "special toy" to keep close at all times. It may be a teddy bear, an elephant, a cat or some other character and usually has a very special name. When lost, it can cause panic and even tragedy.

wear and tear

One problem with security objects is that they have to be present, day in and day out, week after week. Eventually the constant hugging and cuddling takes its toll and the favorite blanket or cloth becomes smelly and ragged. At this point the parent decides, for purposes of hygiene, to wash or repair the much loved object. But for the infant, this may remove the special fragrance, or worn texture, that has become an integral part of the experience of cuddling during moments of insecurity. Even worse is the moment when a parent feels that he must go further and replace the original with a new clean one – a change that is often resisted passionately. Transitional objects become so important to their owners that they acquire the character of intimate companions and develop personal identities. So real do they become that, with some individuals, they are retained for years, and in a few cases even into adulthood.

a maternal instinct

With many small girls, anything super-soft or super-cuddly triggers a strangely inverted response in which the child becomes the symbolic parent and the soft toy becomes the symbolic child. The girl cares for her toy with all the tenderness of a mother protecting her child. Although she is giving rather than receiving security, the cuddling involved still operates successfully as a destressing device.

gender and the brain

How alike are the brains of boys and girls at birth? Does the way in which they are built, or function, result in specific gender characteristics from day one of life outside the womb? Recent investigations suggest that this certainly is the case and, moreover, that such developments begin even earlier, about halfway through pregnancy.

the brain in the womb

When, at about five months old, the testicles of a male fetus start to produce testosterone, there is a significant hormonal impact on the developing tissues of the brain. Enzymes work on the male sex hormones so that they bind with the brain tissue and begin an irreversible transformation. The result of this is that, even as early as the 26th week of pregnancy, it is possible to distinguish a male fetal brain from a female one, and that some of the differences between them are visible to the naked eye.

brain scans

Following substantial new research, brain scans have revealed, for example, that male babies have more asymmetrical brain hemispheres than female babies. They also have more white matter and less gray matter, when compared with female babies. Also, females have more gray matter in the newer parts of the cerebral cortex, while male babies have proportionately more gray matter in the older, more primitive parts of the brain.

Another interesting difference is that, with female brains, there is a greater symmetry in what is called the "higher association cortex." This is the part of the brain most concerned with complex mental processes. Male brains are significantly larger on the left. What little asymmetry there is in female brains reveals that their association cortex is slightly larger on the right. Bearing in mind that the left hemisphere is predominantly concerned with analytical thought, while the right brain is more involved with intuitive thinking, it would seem that perhaps the old wives' tale about the importance of "women's intuition" has, after all, a serious basis in fact.

implications for the future

These early differences in the brains of male and female babies are long lasting and brain-scan tests carried out on adult males and females reveal that they have a long-term impact. During these tests it is possible to see which parts of the brain "light up" (that is to say, become active) when problems are being solved. Females, for example, use both hemispheres at the same time when processing verbal information. Men use only the left hemisphere. When posed with a navigational problem, such as how to reach a particular address, women used mostly the right side of their cerebral cortex, while men employed the left hippocampus. With emotional responses, females mostly use their cerebral cortex. With men, emotional activity is stuck in an older part of the brain – the amygdala. Research has shown that a testosterone surge in infancy appears to enlarge the amygdala, making it visibly bigger in boys' brains. By adulthood, the male amygdala is 16 percent larger than the female's.

If some of these anatomical details are confusing, all one needs to remember is that, from birth and even from before birth, the male and female brains differ in structure, organization and operation. However, although these differences mean that males and females have different thought processes, it does not mean that evolution forces them to act differently, only that they arrive at their conclusions – often perhaps the same conclusions – in different ways. As one brain specialist put it: "The differences in what women and men can do is small; the difference in how they do it is large."

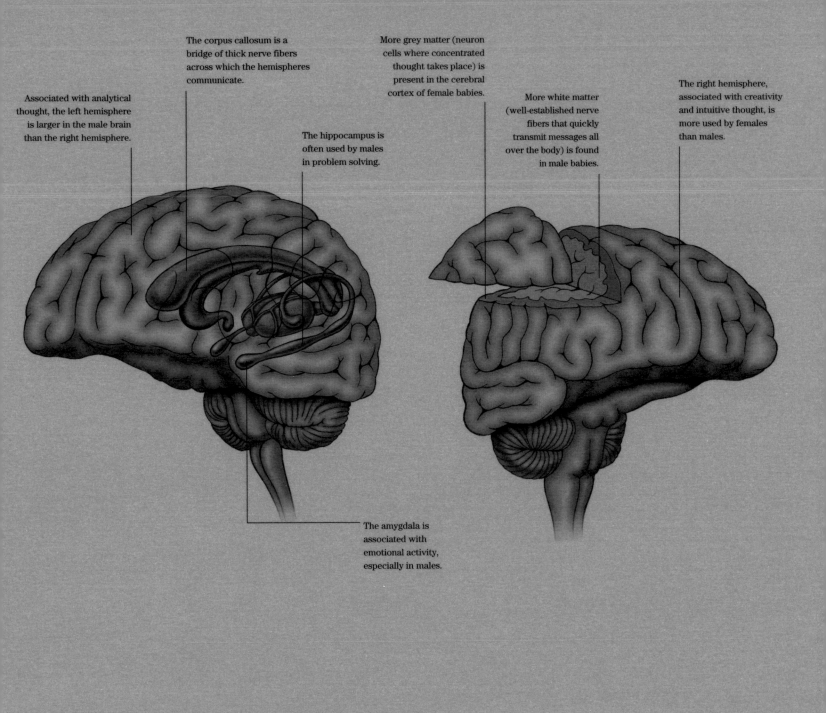

Associated with analytical thought, the left hemisphere is larger in the male brain than the right hemisphere.

The corpus callosum is a bridge of thick nerve fibers across which the hemispheres communicate.

More grey matter (neuron cells where concentrated thought takes place) is present in the cerebral cortex of female babies.

More white matter (well-established nerve fibers that quickly transmit messages all over the body) is found in male babies.

The right hemisphere, associated with creativity and intuitive thought, is more used by females than males.

The hippocampus is often used by males in problem solving.

The amygdala is associated with emotional activity, especially in males.

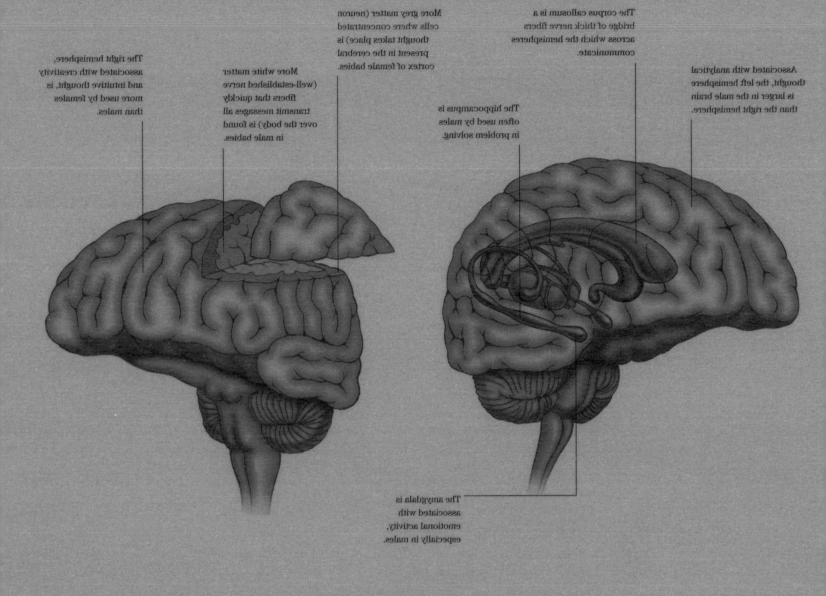

emotional life

Play activities at the baby stage of life are typically solitary, with companions treated largely as "toys." There may be some degree of imitation, when two babies who are sitting near one another engage in parallel play, but this is not true cooperative, social interaction. Parents who notice two babies sitting together and smiling at one another might imagine that they are witnessing an exchange of body language that, in older children and adults, would be a friendly greeting. But at this very early stage, a smile is more likely to be an independent action reflecting the amusement a baby feels at the sight of a fascinating object. If a baby starts to cry her companion may become upset, but this is more likely to be distress caused by an unpleasant sound rather than a sign of sympathy.

Incidentally, a baby reacts to pet animals in the same way, poking a dog or a cat as she would another baby. For this reason, pets are better introduced when the child is much older and can share responsibility for caring for them. A baby should never be left unsupervised with a family pet.

becoming independent

growing confidence

Approaching his second birthday, a toddler stands on the threshold of a time of great wonder and excitement. He still has three years before school starts in earnest, and during this time he is at his most enchanted and enchanting. Given half the chance, he enjoys every day to the fullest as he joyfully explores new levels of language, new muscular skills and new mental challenges. With the helpless stage of babyhood fading into the past, and the serious stage of cultural training still way off in the future, he can wake up every morning with high hopes of having some serious fun and enjoying what may well be the most innocent and happiest days of his entire life.

feelings of insecurity

At around this time, a toddler starts talking to and meeting other children. A child who has been introduced to a variety of situations and who is used to meeting other people from a young age will develop trust and the ability to cope with new experiences. With some children this process is a smooth, gradual one without any major upsets or traumas. With others, however, there are moments of panic and acute distress, with the infant unable to break away from parental protection when expected to do so.

the moment of separation

Infants can be very wary of being left alone with strangers. Even at the age of two, the child may keep one eye on the parent who took them to a playgroup, in case she suddenly disappears. There is a temptation for an adult to wait for her toddler to become engrossed in some game with an exciting new toy and then sneak away when he is not looking. Once this stratagem has been discovered it may appear to the toddler that he has been abandoned, and a panic response may then erupt that it is difficult to control. It makes better sense in the young one's mind if the parent says goodbye with a hug and a kiss and a reassurance that she will soon return to collect him. There may be a moment of crying or panic, but this usually dies down following a swift parental exit and some fascinating diversion created by the playgroup organizer. A short spell of crying is a sign that the child has formed a secure attachment with his parents, not that he is truly insecure.

confidence boosters

There are various ways in which a parent can boost a toddler's confidence. Obviously, offering comfort, love and support at times of distress is one of them. Another is to "let go": allowing a toddler to explore his environment by and for himself is paramount, as long as that environment is safe. In this way, he adds to his experiences and learns to face new challenges head on, finding solutions to problems on his own. Knowing a parent is close at hand encourages him to do this more readily and is an early indication of his emerging independence.

the confident child

The more secure a baby feels in the early stages of life, and the more he trusts his parents, the more self-confident he becomes. His parents prove to him that he is lovable and he therefore develops a sense of self-worth and feels at ease with himself – something he builds on as a toddler. He becomes the one who makes the first moves toward more independent actions. His parents do not have to push him. Instead, he takes the lead, and slowly but surely starts to express himself as a self-confident, outgoing individual, ready to assert himself and accept new challenges.